Accounting and Finance Formulas:

A Simple Introduction

Also by K.H. Erickson

Simple Introductions

Accounting and Finance Formulas
Choice Theory
Corporate Finance Formulas
Econometrics
Financial Economics
Game Theory
Game Theory for Business
Investment Appraisal
Microeconomics

Accounting and Finance Formulas:

A Simple Introduction

K.H. Erickson

Contents

Financial Accounting   6

Management Accounting   15

Financial Management   21

Financial Accounting

Balance sheet

The balance sheet is a statement of the financial position of a business at a single point in time, showing the assets of a firm and the claims on those assets:

Assets = Capital + Liabilities

Assets are the resources held by the business;
Capital is the owner's claim on the business, representing their investment in the business which is considered a separate entity to the owner;
Liabilities are the claims of individuals and organizations, other than the owner, on the business after lending money or supplying goods.

Horizontal balance sheet:

(Non-current assets + Current assets) = (Capital + Non-current liabilities + Current liabilities)

Vertical balance sheet:

Non-current assets + (Current assets − Current liabilities) − Non-current liabilities = Capital

(Current assets − Current liabilities) = Net current assets

Current assets and current liabilities are those relating to the short-run, and non-current assets and non-current liabilities are those held for the long-term operations of the firm.

Profit and loss account (income statement)

Profit (or loss) for a period
= Total revenue for the period − Total expenses incurred in making the revenue

Combining the profit and loss account (income statement) with the balance sheet gives:

Assets = Capital + Profit (or − Loss) + Liabilities

Assets = Capital + (Revenues − Expenses) + Liabilities

Depreciation percentage

$$P = [1 - \sqrt[n]{(R/C)} \times 100\%]$$

P = the depreciation percentage, which shows the proportion of a non-current asset's cost that has been consumed in an accounting period;

n = the useful life of the asset in years;

$\sqrt[n]{}$ = the nth square root;

R = the asset's residual value;

C = the asset's cost or fair value.

Cash flow statement

Cash flows from operating activities
$\pm$ Cash flows from investing activities
$\pm$ Cash flows from financing activities
= Net increase (or decrease) in cash and cash equivalents over a period

$\pm$ = plus or minus, depending on net cash flows.

Cash flow from operating activities are usually the most important for a firm, and it may be calculated indirectly:

Net profit before taxation
+ Depreciation expense
+ Interest expense
± Increase (minus) or decrease (plus) in stock (inventories)
± Increase (plus) or decrease (minus) in debtors (receivables)
± Increase (minus) or decrease (plus) in creditors (payables)
− Interest paid
− Corporation tax paid
− Dividend paid
= Net cash flows from operating activities

Profitability ratios

Return on ordinary shareholders' funds (ROSF)
= (Net profit after taxation and preference dividend / Ordinary share capital plus reserves) x 100%

Return on capital employed (ROCE)
= (Net profit before interest and taxation / Long-term capital employed) x 100%

Long-term capital employed = (Share capital + Reserves + Long-term loans)

Net profit margin
= (Net profit before interest and taxation / Sales revenue) x **100%**

Net profit = Total revenue – Total expenses

Gross profit margin
= (Gross profit / Sales revenue) x **100%**

Gross profit = Sales revenue – Cost of sales

Cost of sales = Opening stock + Stock purchases for a period – Closing stocks held

Efficiency ratios

Average stock (inventory) turnover period
= ([(Opening stock + Closing stock) / 2] / Cost of sales) x **365**

Average settlement period for debtors
= (Trade debtors / Credit sales revenue) x **365**

Average settlement period for creditors
= (Trade creditors / Credit purchases) x 365

Sales revenue to capital employed
= Sales revenue / (Share capital + Reserves + Non-current liabilities)

Sales revenue to capital employed
= Sales revenue / (Total assets – Current liabilities)

Sales revenue per employee
= Sales revenue / Number of employees

Liquidity ratios

Current ratio = Current assets / Current liabilities

Acid test ratio
= Current assets excluding stock / Current liabilities

Cash generated from operations to maturing obligations
= (Cash generated from operations / Current liabilities)

Gearing ratios

Gearing ratio
= [Non-current liabilities / (Share capital + Reserves + Non-current liabilities)] x 100%

Interest cover ratio
= Profit before interest and taxation / Interest payable

Investment ratios

Dividend payout ratio = (Dividends announced for the year / Earnings for the year available for dividends) x 100%

Dividend cover ratio = Earnings for the year available for dividends / Dividend announced for the year

Dividend yield
= (Annual dividend per share / Market price per share) x 100%

Earnings per share = Earnings available to ordinary shareholders / Number of ordinary shares in issue

Where ordinary shares refer to any shares that are not preferred shares and don't have a fixed dividend payment.

Cash generated from operations per share
= Cash made from operations minus any preference dividend / Number of ordinary shares in issue

Price/earnings (P/E) ratio
= Market value per share / Earnings per share

Altman Z score model for financial failure

Altman developed a Z score model that combines financial ratios to predict financial failure, and the model is thought to be accurate up to two years before the bankruptcy occurs:

Z = 1.2a + 1.4b + 3.3c +0.6d +0.999e

a = Working capital / Total assets;
b = Retained profits / Total assets;
c = Profit before interest and taxation / Total assets;

d = Market value of equity / Total book value of liabilities;
e = Sales revenue / Total assets.

Evaluation of the Z scores is as follows:

Z score < 1.81 = firm is likely to fail;
1.81 < Z score < 2.99 = zone of uncertainty;
2.99 < Z score = firm is likely to be financially safe.

With a private firm the Z score model changes to:

Z = 0.717a + 0.847b + 3.107c +0.420d +0.998e

a = (Current assets – Current liabilities) / Total assets;
b = Retained profits / Total assets;
c = Profit before interest and taxation / Total assets;
d = Book value of equity / Total book value of liabilities;
e = Sales revenue / Total assets.

Evaluation of private firm Z scores is as follows:

Z score < 1.23 = firm is likely to fail;
1.23 < Z score < 2.9 = zone of uncertainty;
2.9 < Z score = firm is likely to be financially safe.

Management Accounting

Relevant and irrelevant costs

Relevant costs are those that vary with the decision being considered:

Relevant costs = Opportunity costs + Future outlay costs which vary with the decision being considered

An opportunity cost is the cost of being deprived of the next best option, which will have to be sacrificed in order to proceed with the decision. For example, the opportunity cost for a business project is the alternative project that resources and time could have been used on instead.

Irrelevant costs are those which remain the same irrespective of which decision is made:

Irrelevant costs = Past costs + Future outlay costs which do not vary with the decision being considered

Past (or sunk) costs are irrelevant as they relate to a past decision not the current one;

Irrelevant future outlay costs relate to both non-differential costs and those costs which a business has already committed to and can't be avoided.

Break-even analysis

A firm will break-even and neither make a profit nor suffer a loss at the point where:

Total sales revenue = Total costs

Total sales revenue = Fixed costs + Total variable costs

The point where a firm breaks even is the break-even point (BEP):

Break-even point (BEP) number of units of output = Fixed costs / (Sales revenue per unit – Variable costs per unit)

The difference between the break-even point and the level a business operates at is known as the margin of safety:

Margin of safety = Expected volume of sales – BEP

Job costing

The following two formulas both hold independent of one another, and direct/indirect is unrelated to variable/fixed:

Full costs = Direct costs + Fair share of indirect costs (overheads)

Full costs = Variable Costs + Fixed Costs

If all units of output are the same then:

Cost per unit = Total output cost / Number of units produced

Profit maximization

Profit maximization occurs at the point where:

Marginal sales revenue = Marginal cost of production

Increase in total sales revenue from selling one more unit = Increase in total costs that result from selling one more unit

Firm profits

Economic value added (EVA) calculates whether the generated returns exceed the returns required by investors:

EVA = NOPAT – (R x C)

R = Rate of return required by investors, for example the weighted average cost of capital (WACC);
C = Capital invested, a firm's net assets;
NOPAT = Net operating profit after tax;
NOPAT = EBIT $(1 - T_C)$
EBIT = Earnings before interest and taxes;
T_C = Corporate tax rate.

Actual profit = Budgeted profit + All favourable variances – All adverse variances

Variances

Sales volume variance
= Difference between the actual volume and the budgeted volume in units x Standard contribution for one unit

Contribution = Sales revenue per unit – Variable costs per unit

Standard refers to the budgeted and expected level.

Sales price variance
= Difference between the actual sales revenue and the actual volume at the standard sales price

Direct materials usage variance
= Difference between the actual usage and the budgeted usage for the actual output volume x Standard materials cost

Direct refers to the materials or labour which can be measured by unit of output.

Direct materials price variance
= Difference between the actual materials cost and the actual usage x Standard materials cost

Direct labour efficiency variance
= Difference between the actual labour time and the budgeted labour time for the actual output volume x Standard labour rate

Where the labour rate is the cost of labour per hour.

Direct labour rate variance
= Difference between the actual labour cost and the actual labour time x Standard labour rate

Fixed overhead spending variance = Difference between the actual spending and the budgeted spending on fixed overheads

Financial Management

Investment appraisal

Accounting rate of return (ARR)
= Average annual profit / Average investment to earn that profit

Average annual profit = (Total net profit before depreciation over the project's life / Length of the project in years) – (Total depreciation / Length of the project in years)

Depreciation = Value of the asset at the beginning of the project's life – Value of the asset at the end of the project's life

Straight line depreciation is assumed, where an asset's depreciation is constant over each year of a project.

Average investment = (Book value at start of year 1 + Book value at end of useful life) / 2

If annual cash flows are constant the payback period is:

Payback period (PP)
= Cost of project / Annual cash inflows

If annual cash flows are not constant then the payback period is the year where cumulative cash flows are no longer negative:

Cost of project + Cumulative annual cash inflows $\geq$ 0

Present value discounts cash flows according to the time value of money:

Present value (PV) of the cash flow of year n = Actual cash flow of year n divided by $(1 + i)^n$

Net present value (NPV) = $\sum [R_n / (1 + i)^n]$

n = number of years into the future the cash flow occurs;
R_n = the return in year n;
i = the discount rate;
$\sum [R_n / (1 + i)^n]$ = the sum of all discounted cash flows.

Discount rate = Interest foregone + Inflation + Risk premium

Internal rate of return (IRR) = the value of 'i' in the NPV equation that gives an NPV of zero

Sources of finance

Total internal finance = Short-term internal sources + Long-term internal sources

Short-term internal finance sources = Reduced stock levels + Delayed payment to creditors + Tighter credit control

Long-term internal finance sources = Retained profits

Total external finance = Short-term external sources + Long-term external sources

Short-term external finance sources = Bank overdraft + Debt factoring + Invoice discounting

Long-term external finance sources = Ordinary shares + Preference shares + Loans + Leases

Working capital (WC)

Working capital = Current assets − Current liabilities

Current assets main elements are stocks (inventories), trade debtors (receivables), and cash (both in hand and in a bank). Current liabilities main elements are trade creditors (payables) and bank overdrafts.

Working Capital = Stock + Debtors + Cash – Creditors – Bank overdrafts

Cost minimization

Total costs will be minimized with a certain level of stock, and the economic order quantity (EOQ) model calculates the stock quantity where the total of ordering costs and holding costs are at a minimum:

EOQ = $\sqrt{[(2 \times D \times C) / H]}$

The model assumes that stock is used evenly over time, and is only ordered when the stock level falls to zero.

D = annual demand for the stock item in units;
C = the cost of placing an order for stock;
H = the cost of holding onto one unit of stock for a single year.

Operating cash cycle (OCC)

The operating cash cycle (OCC) is the period between the cash outlay to buy supplies and the receipt of cash from the sale of the goods.

Operating cash cycle = Average stockholding period + Average settlement period for debtors − Average payment period for creditors